Summary & Digest

The Book Thief

Markus Zusak

Dream Digest

Copyright © 2021 All Rights Reserved.

First published in the USA.

This product is licensed for personal usage only and may not be re-sold. Applicable intellectual property (product names, trademarks, etc) featured or referred to within this publication is the property of respective trademark holders and is not endorsed nor affiliated.

CONTENTS

Preface: Our Promise to You

1. Digest of The Book Thief

2. Digest of the Author

3. How Readers React

4. More Interesting Stories

5. Wrap Up Points

6. Group Discussion Questions

About Us

OUR PROMISE TO YOU:

We bring you immaculate reads of *study materials for novels* at exceptionally low prices that do not compromise with quality.

1 DIGEST OF THE BOOK THIEF

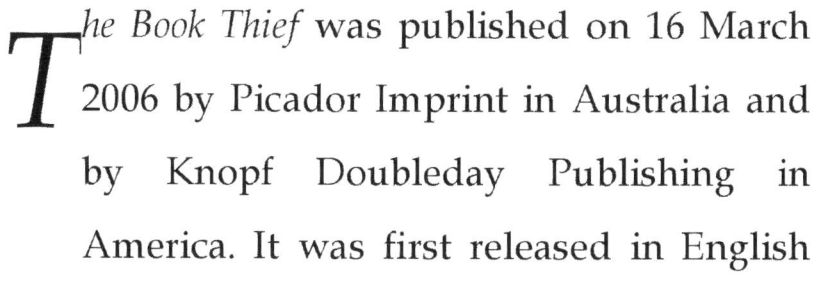

The Book Thief was published on 16 March 2006 by Picador Imprint in Australia and by Knopf Doubleday Publishing in America. It was first released in English and German Language. Until now, it has been translated into more than thirty different languages, including Turkish, French and Italian.

The story of this novel is set in 1939, in a small German town named Molching. It follows the life of a nine-year old girl named Liesel, whose mother gets arrested and taken away. Soon, Liesel's brother dies, and she gets sent away to live with her foster parents. There she becomes friends with a local boy called Rudy, and starts getting into all sorts of mischief. Her favorite activity becomes stealing books from the mayor's house, where her foster mother used to do laundry at. Even though mayor's wife discovers that, she encourages Liesel to continue coming to their house and to take all the books she wants. As she grows up, Liesel learns how to read and write, and becomes fascinated with books.

As the residents of Molching start to feel the first inconvenient effects of the World War II, Liesel's family decide to provide a sanctuary for a Jewish boy named Max Vandenburg, because of the life debt that Liesel's foster father owed to Max's father. They manage to hide Max for several years in their cellar, and during that time, Max becomes a friend with Liesel. He even writes a book for her, entitled *The Standover Man*.

But, once it becomes apparent that the Gestapo will search the house, and that the whole family could perish because of that, Max leaves and Liesel does not see him for months, until he gets transported through the streets of Molching along with the other Jews on their way to Dachau. Liesel decides to walk beside him, and for that both of them get beaten savagely. Because of that, Liesel decides not to take any more books from the mayor's house. However, after a bombing raid in which almost everyone she knew got killed, Liesel ends up living with the mayor and his wife.

One of the most interesting things about *The Book Thief* is that the whole story is narrated by Death itself. As Markus Zusak stated, it took him more than three years to finish this book, because he could not decide whether to tell it from the Death's point of view, or to use Liesel as a narrator. At first, as much as using Death as a storyteller seemed interesting, he hesitated to go through with that idea, because it came off too sadistic and morbid. During this period, Zusak had rewritten the first hundred pages, as he stated, more than a hundred times. Eventually, he managed to make it work once he figured out how the book would end, used bits and pieces of all the previous versions that he had made, and put them together into the final version of this novel.

As an inspiration for this novel, Markus used stories that his parents had told him over the years, particularly the ones about the bombing of Munich, and about Jews being marched through the streets of the town his mother used to live in.

After its release, The Book Thief had spent more than 230 weeks on the New York Times Bestseller list in a row. It received several literary awards, including the National Jewish Book Award, the Association of Jewish Libraries New and Notable Book for Teen

Book Award. Until now, more than a million copies of this novel have been sold, and it is available in hardcover, paperback, e-book, kindle, MP3 and audio CD format.

ⓘ Interesting fact:

When he first started working on The Book Thief, Zusak thought that it would not be such a lengthy novel – he intended it to be about a hundred pages long. But, as he worked on it, he managed to gather a great deal of material, and ended up with a novel that consists of 550 pages in its hardcover and paperback version.

2 DIGEST OF THE AUTHOR

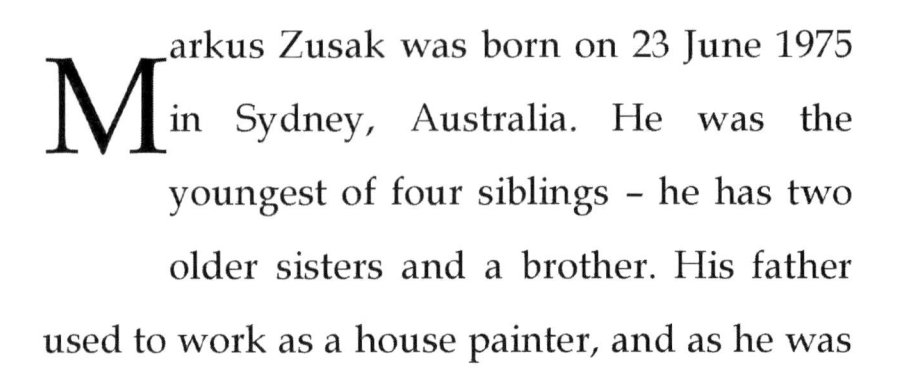

Markus Zusak was born on 23 June 1975 in Sydney, Australia. He was the youngest of four siblings – he has two older sisters and a brother. His father used to work as a house painter, and as he was growing up, Markus thought that he would also become one. But, as he states, each and every time his father would take him to work, he would prove to be quite incompetent in that line of work.

He first started writing short stories when he was sixteen years old, and by the age of eighteen, he had finished his first manuscript for a novel. However, this literary debut by Markus Zusak was never published – simply because Markus never even tried to publish it. As he said, he often had problems with low self-confidence when it comes to writing. Before he decided to become a full-time writer, Markus had worked as an English teacher, and even as a janitor.

Once he finally came up with a novel that he thought was good enough, he tried to publish it, but for seven long years he was faced with nothing but failure. Finally, he published his first novel, The Underdog, and later on three more before he wrote *The Book Thief*. These books were entitled *Fighting Ruben Wolfe*, *When Dogs Cry*, and *The Messenger*. But, despite that, he did not receive any recognition from the literary community until he wrote *The Book Thief* – it was this book that brought him international fame, and made him one of the most successful contemporary Australian authors.

Besides other influences he had as a young, aspiring author, Markus highlights two novels that made the greatest impact on him – *The Old Man and the Sea* by Ernest Hemingway, and *What's Eating Gilbert Grape* by Peter Hedges. And for his greatest achievement yet, *The Book

Thief, he used all the stories he had heard during his childhood from his parents about what it was like living in Munich and Vienna during the World War II.

Today, Markus lives with his wife and their two children in Sydney. He states that he is still plagued by the insecurity when it comes to writing, and that it still presents quite a difficult task for him. The way he deals with it is a set of his daily routines – Markus likes to write during a specific time of day, because in the morning his self-confidence is at its lowest, and he also doesn't like working late at night. He always works in the same room and on the same worktable.

⊙ Interesting fact:

During his adolescence, Markus did not like to be referred to by his name, because he did not like it very much. During that period, he would go by his middle name, Frank.

[Help us improve your experience.](#)

3 HOW READERS REACT

The commercial success that *The Book Thief* achieved speaks for itself when it comes to the reception that this book encountered by the audience. More than a million sold copies throughout the world surely is a figure that cannot be argued with. As it turned out, the critics who reviewed it were also full of praise, and felt that *The Book Thief* indeed is a remarkable piece of literary work.

Of course, the most fascinating feature of this novel is the fact that it is being narrated by Death itself. As many critics, like Kirkus Reviews, Bookmarks Magazine and Nataliya from the Goodreads noticed, this detail gave the book a striking, eerie atmosphere, and made it stand out from all the other books on holocaust.

But, the idea to use Death as a storyteller itself surely would not suffice by itself to make *The Book Thief* one of the bestselling titles – it was the way Markus Zusak masterfully managed to find the right voice for his spooky storyteller that made it great. And, according to Time Magazine and AudioFile, Markus managed to do that by maintaining the right distance from the events that Death takes part in without any pride or joy whatsoever, with subtle dose of indifference and dark, bitter humor that makes this heart wrenching story bearable to read.

Another thing that caught the attention of numerous reviewers is that Zusak made a novel in which books are regarded as a treasure. The New York Times and Janet Maslin agreed that his was something that simply cannot be ignored. Even though there were those who felt that this book was not the greatest choice for teenagers and young adults due to its grim subject, The New York Times stated that *The Book Thief* is a book that offers and finds hope at the end, despite all the atrocities its characters face, and that makes it great for any audience.

❗ Interesting fact:

Many reviewers pointed out the magnificent performance by Allan Corduner, the actor who narrated the audio version of *The Book Thief*. According to them, the way that he portrayed Death greatly contributed to the overall atmosphere of this version of the novel.

4 MORE INTERESTING STORIES

Even though Markus was born in Australia, his parents were from Germany and Austria, and both of them had experienced all the horrors and the atrocities of war firsthand. That's why Markus had such a great starting point for writing a story about that period of German history. But, as he had stated on several occasions, he did not want to write a book about holocaust – his original intention was to write a universal story about human kindness and cruelty, loyalty and betrayal. In fact, he thought that the way he wrote *The Book Thief* was so strange that no one would even want to read it, so he wrote this book for himself.

Because this novel is being narrated from the Death's point of view, Markus wrote it a bit differently than other books – he wanted to describe what would the world we live in look like to Death, and that would be slightly different than humans see it.

Although some writers claim that writing

process is easy for them, and once they conceive characters the story almost rolls out all by itself, Markus stated that it was never like this for him – in fact, he always points out that writing is a traumatic and difficult work for him. Unlike other writers, Markus gladly discusses anything with the public - even the books he is currently working on. He is quite aware that almost all other authors dread from it, but he states that he doesn't mind talking about it.

The commercial success that *The Book Thief* achieved resulted in movie adaptation of this book. The movie based on it was released on 8 November 2013. It was directed by Brian Percival, and the screenplay for it was written by Michael Petroni. The movie was filmed at several different locations in Germany, such as the city of Berlin and a town named Görlitz, because the novel is set in an imaginary town called Molching. During the shooting of the movie, Markus Zusak visited the set and got acquainted with the crew while they were shooting in Berlin.

The roles of Liesel's foster parents were played by Geoffrey Rush, an Academy Award winner, and Emily Watson, an Academy Award nominee. Emily Watson was also nominated for the Best Supporting Actor at the Satellite Awards for the role she played in this movie. The role of Liesel was given to a young actress Sophie Nélisse, who won the Breakthrough Performance Award at the 2013 Satellite Awards for her performance in *The Book Thief*.

When it comes to characters from *The Book*

Thief, Markus Zusak always points out Rudy as his favorite one, and often states that one of his favorite moments in the book is the one when Rudy paints himself black so that he would look like Jesse Owens, who had won four gold medals at the Olympic Games in Berlin in 1936. Although he wrote Rudy as a fictional character, Markus admits that he drew inspiration for this character from the personality of his father.

Interesting fact:

Markus' favorite free-time activity is surfing. He states that some of his best childhood memories are connected with riding waves, and that his brother was a big support and encouragement for him when he was still struggling to learn how to surf.

5 WRAP UP POINTS

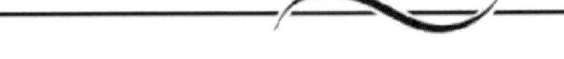

- *The Book Thief* is penned by Markus Zusa.
- The story revolves around Liesel and the childhood she had spent during World War II in Germany.

- *The Book Thief* is narrated from the point of view of Death itself.
- After Liesel's mother gets taken away, she moves to a town named Molching to live with her foster parents.
- Her foster parents decide to take in a Jewish boy named Max, and hide him in the cellar.
- Liesel and her friend Rudy start to get into all sorts of mischief, one of which being stealing books from the mayor's house.
- Zusak states that his intention was not to write a book strictly about holocaust, but about human compassion and cruelty.
- The book was greatly accepted by the audience, and there were more than a million copies sold worldwide.

- The movie adaptation of *The Book Thief* was released in 2013.
- In the movie, the roles of Liesel's foster parents were played by Geoffrey Rush and Emily Watson.

6 GROUP DISCUSSION QUESTIONS

1. If you could see things from the Death's point of view, how would you describe

the events that took place during the World War II?

2. How do you think all those events looked like from the perspective of a nine-year old girl?

3. Why do you think that the mayor's wife did not mind Liesel stealing books from her home?

4. Why do you think Markus Zusak thought that no one would want to read this book?

5. Do you think that the people who think that this book is inappropriate for teenagers are wrong, and why?

ABOUT US

Dream Digest was inspired by an effort to provide immaculate reads at exceptionally low prices. We offer a unique view to provide simple answers to many readers alike – *academically driven study materials for novels*. Formulated for high-efficiency learning, our publication aims to help you learn materials quickly and effectively to determine if the next book is right for you.

Printed in Great Britain
by Amazon